NEAR DEATH CAT

NEAR DEATH CAT

Nine Lives with a Speed Bump at The End

Charles Kelly

Illustrations by Kee Rash

ASCLEPIAN IMPRINTS LTD.

Copyright © 2016 by Charles Kelly

Near Death Cat: Nine Lives With a Speed Bump at The End
Asclepian Imprints Ltd.

ISBN 978-0-9858911-9-0

First Edition
All Rights Reserved
Story by Charles Kelly.
Illustrations and design by Kee Rash.

Printed in the USA

This book is a work of fiction

*If man could be crossed with the cat
it would improve man, but deteriorate the cat.*

— MARK TWAIN

TABLE OF CONTENTS

The Fatal Tuna 1
Weird Tunnel 3
My Rotten Life 7
Flying Fur 10
Vets from Hell 13
The Crystal Garbage Cans 15
Cat in Extremis 18
Showtime 21
Fizz and Fizzle 23
The Gizzards of Knowledge 25
The Gizmos of Salvation 29
Back for The Business 33
World of Hurt 35
Bad Times 40
Hogarth's Lives 43

Rocking Chairs 45
In A Glass Darkly 49
Open Ticket 53
The Sparks Fly Upward 56
Road Trip 61
A Metaphor I Didn't Like 65
The Funny Farm 68
A Breath of No Air 72
Loss Leader 75
Cat and Catastrophe 79
There From Here 83
The Big One 88
How this book came to be 93
Credits 95

The Fatal Tuna

Shortly before the first of my nine lives was squashed like a mouse on a snare drum, I had a premonition I wasn't long for this world.

Let me set the scene. It was a cool desert morning, the moist smells of cacti and paloverde issuing through the kitchen window. My owner was at work in his office far down the hall, and I had slipped into the half-open fridge in his adobe casita in El Macho, Arizona. My mission: to filch the contents of a half-eaten can of tuna.

I had made it onto the first shelf, was balanced precariously upon the wire tines, and was just extending my right forepaw toward the shelf above—and the tuna—when my brain was suffused with a fatal vision. I saw my body stretched out on the floor, whiskers bent and crumpled, little Xs where my eyes should have been, a narrow tendril of cat-drool extending from the left corner of my jaws.

Just then, my forepaw struck the can and the horrible vision became reality. CRASH. BANG. A projectile of metal can and tuna arrowed into my cringing forehead, and I knew no more.

There I was, just as I'd imagined: lying on my kinked tail on the cold Saltillo tile, my fur splotched with Chunk Light Tuna in Oil. I had a look in my eyes as if I'd just pushed my whiskers beyond the Veil and discovered that God is a cocker spaniel with a bad attitude.

Weird Tunnel

The odd thing was that I felt no pain. That surprised me. The kid next door had once bounced an empty Budweiser can off my dome, and it hurt like 60 million bucks. The impact raised a welt big as a hawser, and I cried the blues for two weeks, with my head going oom-pah-pah, oom-pah-pah. And that was just an empty can, not one half-loaded with liquid-logged tuna.

The other funny thing was that I wasn't in my body. I can now give you such a juicy description of my battered carcass because I was floating above it. I was high on the wall, in an area where my owner Jed had removed a bullfighter painting and replaced it with a Museum-of-Modern-Art poster of fruit in a crystal bowl.

Speaking of Jed, the hellacious clang of the falling tuna can had immediately summoned him from down the hallway, where he had been putting in his daily stint composing messages for greeting cards. He leaned over my scrawny physique with his lips trembling, as if he had just lost his only friend in town.

I suppose you might say he had. El Macho, Arizona, is a pretty place, but the main entertainment is country dancing and crushing beer cans against your forehead down at the Round-Up Bar. It's no place for a gentle soul like Jed, who is so nonviolent he wouldn't split an infinitive if it threatened him with a butcher knife.

Jed is a displaced person, you see. He would have been happy growing up in New York City or San Francisco, where people understand the artistry of greeting-card slogans. Instead, he was raised in a small town in Iowa where creative endeavors are limited to poking a rake at the chain of the local Mobil sign, trying to get some rhythm into its swing. Mischance landed him here in El Macho and here he stayed, an isolated genius.

Such was the human who was leaning over me at this moment, his nubby dressing gown flapping in the breeze from the window, his hands making flipping motions of distress. He didn't stay that way for long. Within seconds, he leaped to the butcher-block counter to capture the kitchen phone and jangle up the local cat hospital.

His call delivered, Jed stood helplessly, his cheeks moist with bulbous tears that exploded like water balloons whenever they struck a projection on his face: his well-chewed mustache, his knobby chin. I was feeling pretty bad myself, not so much for the cat down there on the floor as for Jed.

Fact was, I didn't want to leave him to the tender mercies of the can-crunchers and gas-station artists of this world. But what could I do? So far as my body was concerned, I seemed to have vacated the premises, and it didn't look like my lease was going to be renewed.

I was pondering all this from my perch near the ceiling fixtures. As I did, I turned my eyeballs upward the way I do when I'm thinking deeply.

At this precise moment, I saw something I'd never seen before. A swirling white tunnel had formed where the wall met the ceiling. It put me in mind of the White Tornado that used to clean bathrooms in TV commercials, but it was not nearly so aggressive. In fact, it was an inviting, misty passageway into some unknown area of reality.

It moved toward me as I took one last glance at Jed and that played-out cat down there. Jed was still weeping, pumping his hands in frustration as he waited for the catambulance (a Galacian term the feline hospital preferred to "cat ambulance"). The cat was stiff and stark. While I couldn't identify with the cat emotionally, I didn't want to leave, because I somehow knew I had a vital stake in the outcome.

However, the tunnel was beckoning. Really, it was more than beckoning. It impelled me inside and up. And so I went. Suddenly I was sailing into space, preparing to dare greatly beyond the reach of feline experience, to go boldly where cat had never gone, to seek and explore unknown worlds where cat had never set paw.

My Rotten Life

I was moving faster and faster, so fast that my tail was whipping in the wind and throwing off sparks like a downed electrical line. Far off at the end of the tunnel, I could see a bright, white light that resounded with melodious wind chimes, serving me up an aural experience much like celestial Muzak.

I was concentrating on the music so much that I almost didn't notice I had a fellow traveler. Moving right along with me was a being who was not a tuna-can-befuddled soul, but an enlightened presence, a spiritual advisor oozing wisdom and internal harmony.

This being seemed to have neither gender nor species. That is, I couldn't tell if it was a he or a she, a warthog, a human, or Galapagos turtle. No, this was simply a translucent entity that appeared to be long and flowing, a clear plastic shower curtain exuding love.

The love part freaked me out, because I hardly deserved it. I had never been a perfect cat. Jed had named me Dundee Blinky, but my middle name was "Bad." As Shower Curtain and I flew through the tunnel, I was reminded of this, because I began to see scenes of my past life.

I'd been a junkyard cat before Jed plucked me, pneumonia-ridden and starving, from a roadside patch of weeds and nursed me back to health with hot tomato soup and stewed yogurt. Before Jed, I'd been a terror. Born in the back seat of a rusted-out El Camino, thrown early in life on my own devices, I'd carried a grudge against the world that I worked out in a variety of grotesque ways.

As the scenes of my life played out, I was shocked to see how violent I'd been. I was always fighting. I'd pick on any cat, no matter how big, and call him out. Many of these cats didn't want to fight. Some were Zen cats, some were Quaker cats, some were cats whose ancestors had gone to Canada to avoid being drafted as troop cats during the Vietnam War.

None of this mattered to me. I'd never been happy unless my teeth were clogged with some other cat's hair and flesh. That gave me terrible breath, but it sated my fury and reminded me I was the toughest cat in El Macho.

As my life continued in instant replay, though, I recalled that I hadn't always been considered the toughest cat in El Macho. I saw now how I had earned the title, in the most despicable way possible.

At the time, the king of the tough-pile was a tomcat named Hannibal. Word was that his forebears came from Hannibal, Missouri, and I guess they grow their cats mean and mangy in that part of the world, because Hannibal had claws like salad forks, a smell like a ratty buffalo hide, and a disposition so vicious that he had to sneak up on dry cat food to keep from scaring it away.

I knew that eventually Hannibal and I would have to meet. He was looking for me, just like I was looking for him. As it happened, we ran into each other by accident. I came around a corner into the back yard of a little clapboard house inhabited by a broken-down country-western singer, and there was Hannibal, digging through a collection of mildewed Tater Tots from a spilled garbage can.

He saw me immediately, or I would have ducked back around the corner. I wanted to be careful about choosing the circumstances of our claw-fest, but now I could see this wasn't going to happen. He hissed at me and squared up to fight. I got my fur up into battle position, too, but I certainly wasn't going to jump right in. Fortunately, he gave me an out.

"So I gotcha, ya little mouser," he gloated. "I hear you been marking my territory. Guess you know I don't stand for anybody else's pee where I do my business. Are you game, or do I have to chase your skinny butt all the way to Yuma to get you to fight?"

"Nobody chases me anywhere," I said, though I was getting a scratchy feeling way down in my throat. Hannibal looked as big as a sofa and smelled like pee-yew.

He contemplated one of his broken claws, a smug purr rumbling deep in his throat. He wasn't satisfied with just getting it done, he wanted to torture me. "Fine," he said. "Let's see if your nerve will last the night. Why don't you and me get together tomorrow morning, nine sharp, behind the Esso station? I'll bring some kitties along to enjoy the fun."

Flying Fur

"**S**ounds perfect to me," I said, and I turned as if to go. I glanced back over my shoulder. Hannibal had fallen for the ploy, presenting me his back as he stuck his sniffer back into the garbage. I took two swift bounds and caught him behind the right ear with a sucker punch that sent him staggering like a slam-dancer mesmerized by mescal.

I followed up quickly, plastering his eyes with chunks of Tater Tot. As I got in another whack, I explained the situation. "I just remembered I couldn't make it tomorrow, so I thought I'd get it on right now." I continued my assault, jerking his tail and swinging him into position for a head-butt right in the schnozz. "I hope you understand."

The move left Hannibal a battered mess. It ended our battle right there, but it was a dirty thing to do.

Some of the other stuff I'd pulled was equally bad. I'd once known a mouse who managed to eat regularly only by springing mousetraps and stealing the cheese. I'd fiddled with one of those traps, replacing a hunk of cheese with a

yellow jawbreaker, then hiding in the weeds next to the trap. Before long, here he came, and I chuckled like a nut when he chomped down on that hard sphere and rearranged his dental work.

That's not all. I'd once had a grudge against the bulldog next door, and I regurgitated a pincushion-sized hairball into his Gravy Train. I stirred it in so deep he never knew what hit him. When he bit down on that thing, he choked like he was going to cough up his gizzard, and he probably would have passed out if his owner hadn't given him mouth-to-mouth, sucking some of the hairy hunk into his own throat, causing him to hurl his breakfast.

And all the time this was going on, all through this mean part of my life, I laughed! Now, as I watched these scenes rerunning, it all seemed so sick and vicious. What could I have been thinking? I had spent my life in very selfish ways, ways that involved entirely too much regurgitation.

I had been catty. I had preened myself all the time instead of licking people's faces. I'd tomcatted around at night, playing fast and loose with the affection of many kitties. How many lives had I hurt? Why had I spent so much of my time spitting up hair when I could have used that time to do good deeds?

Well, that was over. There was nothing I could do about that now. But one thing I could do was change the way I acted in the future. I looked at Shower Curtain and tried to exude a little love of my own. A little repentance. A little honesty.

"No more saliva-covered jokes for me," I swore. "No more fighting. From now on, I'm going to leap into people's laps at every opportunity, rub up against their legs, groom them with my tongue. My fellow beings, human and animal, will see a new Dundee!"

Then, suddenly, it occurred to me that that wasn't so. They weren't going to see a new Dundee or an old Dundee. Because I was back there on Jed's kitchen floor, coded-out, my consciousness level so far below the alpha and delta states that the alphabet didn't reach down that far. I was colder than an Eskimo's butt, hollower than a hog-trough after dinner, goner than last July.

Vets from Hell

The veterinarians tried everything to save me. Everything they were capable of doing, that is.

When Jed heard tires hissing in the dirt outside and gravel spitting on the front door, he rushed out. There was the fully equipped catambulance: a Toyota four-banger pickup with a crumpled rear fender and, in the truck bed, a cat cage that hadn't been hoovered out since Persia was a kit.

Two pimply faced vet attendants rushed into the kitchen, gently shoveled me onto a chunk of cardboard ripped from a packing carton, and hauled tail for the front door. I was told they did their best to inject my carcass into the cat cage. It was just bad luck that the cardboard chunk was slippery, so that they accidently rocketed my already-battered head into the side of the truck bed, raising lumps on my lumps and causing my eyeballs to spin like beanie-propellers in a high wind.

Such mishaps aside, they did get me to the cat hospital a half-mile away in 40 minutes flat, stopping only twice—once for gasoline and once for Hearty Burgers at the Gristle Grill.

True, it wasn't lunchtime yet, but anyone on a mission of mercy this vital was bound to work up an appetite.

There were two vets at the hospital, already outfitted for surgery in high-rayon, loose-hanging Hawaiian shirts that swept over and far below their bellies and provided sanitary protection from the mayonnaise marks their fingers had left on the crotch areas of their designer jeans.

They were natives of Hamburg, Germany, named Hans and Willi, and they allowed Jed to stand by as they did their business, so later he was able to describe the whole scene to me. It wasn't pretty.

The Crystal Garbage Cans

Back on earth, things were looking grim, but up here in the wild blue yonder, I was swinging. Shower Curtain and I had swept right out of the end of the tunnel into the higher reaches of the universe, and I was feeling calm, cool and collected.

Because I didn't seem to be in my body anymore, I'd accepted my demise, and was scoping out a possible new career. Could I, for instance, get the Great Being to turn me into a Cat-Sized Shower Curtain so that I could sweep around the universe emitting Muzak?

If I had to make a good showing at a job interview, I was ready. All I had to do was de-emphasize the disgusting aspects of my personality and stress the positive, such as my knowledge, through Jed, of dozens and dozens of greeting-card slogans ("Happy Burpday: Here's a Six-Pack to Help You Celebrate.")

While I was mulling all this, the air was whistling through my fur and the sky was clear. Below, I could see the craggy outlines

of beautiful peaks and heavy-limbed trees rich with glowing fruits.

I turned and fixed an eye on Shower Curtain.

"Where are we going, O Translucent One?" I asked. "We've been sweeping for quite some time now, and my paws are itchy for hard ground."

The being emitted a sound something like O-ALLA-HOUM, O-ALLA-HOUM, which I took to be either a chant of praise to the All-Powerful Creator of the Universe or a symptom of advanced bowel problems. I didn't want to ask which. That would have continued the pattern of my nasty life. And it wasn't fair, anyway, because Shower Curtain was a heck of an entity. He continued to pump out love like a busted utility pipe. So what if he had gas-filled intestines?

Besides, I needed him. He was my guide to the unknown territory we were moving into. The surroundings were getting more and more mysterious. We were moving upward at a greater rate now, cutting across fields of energy that swirled around us like smoke from a burning Subaru.

My spirit hummed with high-frequency screeches and moans as we flew through the air. I had begun to wonder whether I would spend eternity sounding like a radio tuned between stations when our destination hove into view. It was beautiful.

Imagine the loveliest back alley in the universe: crystal garbage cans as tall as cathedrals with artistically dented sides that rivaled the work of Titian and Michelangelo, standing among carefully arranged piles of litter—fresh fish, newly opened boxes of catnip, balls of vari-colored yarn that no-one, cat or human, had ever played with. Fresh hot Tater Tots right out of some celestial microwave.

In we swept among the garbage cans, straight toward the most sumptuous one of all. It was lying on its side, big enough to encompass a fleet of Mack trucks, its interior glowing like a corrugated diamond, vibrating with a sound that soothed me like the world's best belly rub.

We went right in. The bottom part of the crystal can was flat and equipped with silver bleachers. Shower Curtain and I took our seats, and I sensed that other beings were in the bleachers around us. I couldn't actually see them. They appeared to be translucent. I thought of them as Beings of Light. Why, I don't know. Perhaps I was just lightheaded.

I waited for the show to begin, figuring (correctly, as it turned out) that it would be amazing. But I almost didn't get to see it. Death was the ticket in, and the people I'd left behind—Jed, in particular—didn't want to let me go.

Cat in Extremis

Back in Arizona, Hans and Willi were giving me the treatment.

Hans tossed me and the slab of cardboard on the examining table as if serving up a pizza. Then he put on a dingus like a miner's headlamp and checked my vital signs.

"Hey, Jed," said Hans, his big, testosterone-starved breasts rippling under his Hawaiian shirt, "this cat has caught a big smashen-bangen on the noggin. What goes on? He French-kiss a speeding semi?"

Jed stepped forward shakily. "A tuna can fell on his head. Can you tell me, is it serious?"

Willi flipped my left forepaw. It swung loose in regular sweeps, like an upside-down metronome. With great satisfaction, he chewed chunks of schnitzel trapped in his luxuriant mustache. "I would say serious as a heart attack, except his head, it's all this way and that way, which you don't get with a heart attack." He glanced significantly at Hans. "Looks like he got caressed by an auto-smasher, or maybe a brick house fell on him from a great height."

Jed's lips trembled. "It's just a tuna can, I swear. Can you do anything?"

Hans and Willi looked at each other. Hans harrumphed. "We can do something, of course. You see the sign outside, Special Cat Hospital? That's us. We got the latest equipment, and our knowledge is about as advanced as you can get without being visited by aliens. So, can we get on with the diagnosis?"

Poor Jed. His mouth moved, but he was afraid to say more. He backed into a corner, bumping against an old hydraulic jack. He looked around and realized the place was jammed with junk—cast-off toasters, an antiquated pop machine, ancient fireplace tools, rusted-out generators, worn-out electrical cables, other grotesque machinery.

Hans was fingering my wound. "Hmmm. Some brain matter here—not much, considering a cat this size. Hey, Jed, this cat…was he a dummkopf, maybe, a stupe?"

The vet waved a hand. "I'm just asking, professional, because if there's more bone here than brain, maybe the damage doesn't go too deep. Though I got to say this cat looks like a gorilla used him for batting practice."

Jed straightened his shoulders. "It was…it was, a tuna-can accident," he insisted. "You've got to treat him."

Hans looked miffed. "Hey, we treat him, okay? It's just, you got to base treatment on the damage, and there's plenty damage here, he looks like an elephant's settee. Willi, let's try to get a rise out of this cat. Usual methods."

Willi plucked an onion from the top of an antiquated Hotpoint range, and waved it under my nostrils. My mucous membranes contracted, but my eyes remained zoned-out.

Hans sighed. "Crap. An all-system shutdown. Willi, we must now proceed to the next stage. Bop him on the funny bone. Give him a good clout."

Willi complied, cracking a large knuckle into my right foreleg just above the joint, trying to compress the chuckle nerve and send a jangle through my leg and shoulder. No dice. My address was still Limpville.

Showtime

In the crystal garbage can, things were heating up. At first, I thought the Beings of Light were waiting for some performance to begin, like I was. As it turned out, *they* were the show. One by one, except for Shower Curtain, they got up and formed a line, leading to me.

Now they weren't translucent. They revealed patterns and textures. One was plaid, one was gingham, one was corduroy, still another was nubby poplin. For each, the pattern represented the Being's particular emotion—mild irritation, giddiness, uneasiness, goofiness, worry (sometimes a specific worry, such as concern that a piece of lettuce was stuck in the Being's teeth).

Tremendous relief washed over me as I observed the Beings. I had often experienced these emotions, but had thought them cheap. Now I saw that they were, in fact, the most powerful drives in the universe. It wasn't heroism or determination that decided the fate of nations; it was some national leader's worry that he had lettuce stuck in his teeth.

Now the first Being moved closer, and I could see its gizzard glowing, changing shape, expanding, pictures forming in it—the most amazing scenes. I strained on my forepaws to get a good look at the celestial movie dancing across the Being's internal organ.

Wow! Things were—

But then the picture fuzzed up. I realized that I still had one paw on the brink of death, one clawing to get my life back. At this point, I could go either way.

Fizz and Fizzle

Hans flapped his arms, his Hawaiian shirt galloping around his mushy torso, his untrimmed eyebrows flipping in frustration.

"Options, we ain't got many left," he said. "We can try the Fizzy Cola, I guess. That worked once with a dachshund. Shortened him up a little bit and made him stagger sideways, but it got him back."

He swung a beefy arm at a collection of equipment cluttering a shelf behind Willi's head. "We'll give it a swing, Willi. Capture down a hypodermic and cop a cola for me." He cut a sideways glance at Jed and burped a chuckle. "Nothing but the best for Mr. Cat. Yes, sir, we'll give him the treatment. Extremo Delicto."

Willi reached above his head and extracted a hypo from the midst of a pile of machine parts. He pulled a Fizzy Cola from the pop machine, uncapped it and inserted the needle, drawing a hissing cargo of cola into the chamber. Hans snatched the hypo and punched it into my jugular, pumping the injection home.

"There," he said with satisfaction, withdrawing the needle. "That should fizz his blood, pop his flivver, and jump-start his heart in seconds flat." He coughed. "Anyway, it will if it works."

It didn't. My body, loose as a wet noodle, continued to do an excellent imitation of a corpus delicti. Hans threw up his hands.

"It is what it is," he said. "Dueling with angels and devils is what we been doing, and now here's what we got for it: defeat. Game's over. This cat is down the road."

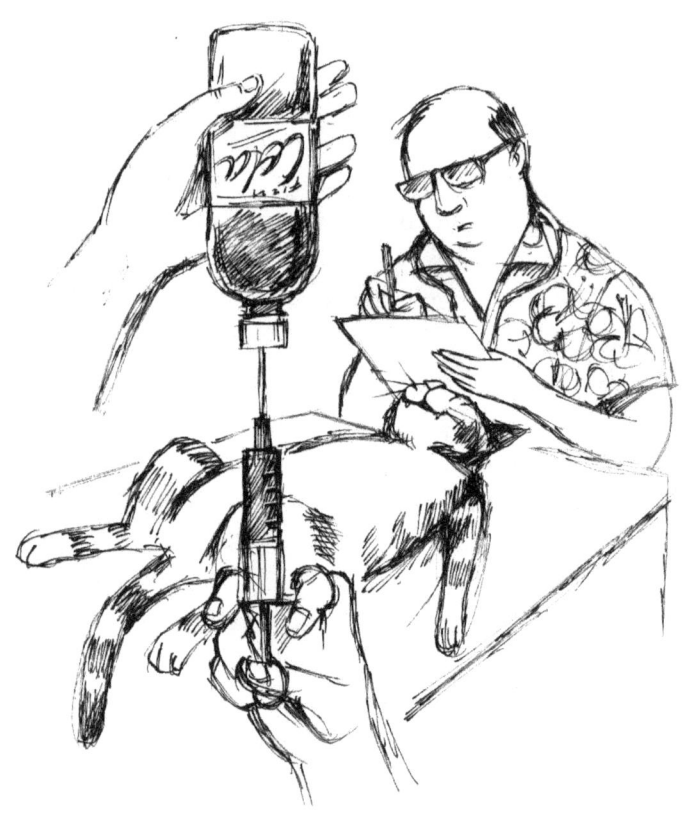

The Gizzards of Knowledge

The first Being moved even closer. I could see the intestinal walls of his gizzard glowing like a TV screen slick with digestive juice. Gee, I thought, that must give him a primo bellyache. Wonder what his bill is for Pepto?

Then the gizzard bounced right out of his belly and headed for my face. It stopped two inches from my nose. I saw a room, a glowing fire, a large mahogany desk, a wall calendar for the year 2023. What I had taken for an alimentary TV screen was really a portal into the future.

Behind the desk sat a cat in a Brooks Brothers suit, button-down white shirt and a repp tie, his paws folded decisively, his whiskers twitching with sincerity. On the front of the desk was the Great Seal of the United States. My god! A cat had been elected president! Maybe there was still hope for Sarah Palin.

I bent forward, eager to hear how this cat of the future would deal with national problems. But before he could speak the intestinal-wall TV flickered again and I was seeing the problems for myself: street cats in Seattle screeching for their supper, cats rioting in Los Angeles, cats picketing in Chicago, waving signs that demanded better prowling conditions ("Keep the Dog Locked Up!" "Better Scraps!" "More Half-Empty Milk Bottles!").

America seemed to be concerned solely with the problems of cats. This was a significant change. Something told me the Republicans were no longer in charge.

Abruptly, the first Being sucked his gizzard back into his vitals and another stepped forward, flashing his own stomach-TV at me. Now I could see what was happening. I was getting a series of stomach shows, a grab bag of videos of the future and what it portended for humans as well as cats.

I bent my attention to the gizzard-show. I was suffused by a sense of wonder and also by the desperate hope that I could get inside information on catnip futures, which could set me up for life. (I kept forgetting that my life, as I knew it, had ended.)

All in all, nine beings trooped by me, showing me a variety of visions of the future. Here's what I saw:

GIZZARDS ONE THROUGH THREE

I saw a troop convoy moving through Iran, or possibly Indiana (my knowledge of geography and terrain is limited). The soldiers wore strange, transparent headgear, like fishbowls turned upside down. This puzzled me. Then I picked up a few blips of sound, one of the troopers complaining, "Damn fishbowls…when are we going to get helmets again?"

My interpretation: The world would see severe shortages of metal in the future, many pet fish would be homeless, and hostilities would bring heartache and destruction to Iran (or possibly Indiana).

I saw nuclear-bomb-like explosions occurring in various parts of the globe.

The settings were all different. Sometimes the explosions would occur in open areas and I would see small animals—gophers, woodchucks, ferrets—flipping out of their holes and somersaulting through the air, while the leaves of nearby trees fried and shriveled like potato chips. In other cases, the explosions would occur in coffee shops, causing coffee drinkers to vaporize and become one with the brew they were ingesting—Kona Coast and Blue Mountain varieties usually, though in the cheaper shops, there was a marked instance of Irish Cream. In still other cases, the nuclear blasts destroyed theme parks that were closed for the night, or gas stations that had been converted into boutiques, then failed due to a shortage of floppy hats.

My interpretation: In the future, no place would be safe, not even the area next to the sugar and cream packets in a coffee shop, which normally is the most strategic place to be.

I also saw black cats in veils and long, sweeping garments, trooping through the streets of a major city. There was rubble all around, as well as burned-out buildings and devastated vehicles. There were no people on the streets. The cats coughed and shivered as they moved.

My interpretation: Except for the cats and the clothing, this was a present-day scene in Bayonne, New Jersey.

GIZZARDS FOUR THROUGH SIX

These were scenes of a plague devastating the earth. I saw vision after vision of people with terrible hacking coughs and that ache-all-over feeling, factories spewing over-the-counter nostrums but never able to keep up with the need, people deciding they were too sick to go to work, then slipping out a few hours later to go to a movie. It was horrible. Could this be how the world would end, with everyone watching matinees and sniffling into their handkerchiefs? I fervently hoped not.

GIZZARDS SEVEN THROUGH NINE

These were scenes of economic chaos: I saw people maxing out credit cards issued by pet-food establishments, ordering neon pot holders and left-handed divot replacers from advertisements sent with their phone bills, people going into cute little shops to buy $5 cupcakes they could have baked at home for 11 cents. What terrible future aberration in mass thinking would account for these developments? I couldn't fathom it.

But my lesson in the future was not over. As the last of the nine entities folded his gizzard and passed from my sight, I turned to Shower Curtain. The Being was glowing now with some inner information that he wanted to transmit, though, in my ignorance, I feared he was about to emit swamp gas. Wordlessly, he informed me that the future was not set in stone, that it could be changed by the humblest creature on earth, a bad cat. Me.

The Gizmos of Salvation

All the time I was watching the future, one question nagged at me. Why was I, a noggin-knocked feline, being shown all this?

Now, Shower Curtain told me. Again, he projected the thoughts into my mind.

"These visions of the future, all these horrible things you have seen, they won't necessarily happen," he said.

"Hmmm," I replied. "So I guess they weren't really visions of the future, were they?"

"Well," he said uneasily. "They were and they weren't. It's complicated. They will happen if you don't change your attitude and start doing things differently."

"What? Are you kidding? You think what one cat does can change the future? Isn't that a little egotistical, not to say narcissistic? How come all the nice things cats and humans have done for each other over the centuries haven't changed the world up to now?"

"Look," said Shower Curtain. "I don't know, okay? A lot of stuff happens above my head. I don't ask questions. It might affect my job security. I'm just supposed to exude love and give you directions. And, if you really want to know, I'm also supposed to be mysterious. So lay off."

I pawed my whiskers. "Why should I trust you? You fiddled with the pictures, probably upsetting a whole lot of people in Bayonne. Maybe what's really going to happen in the future is that people are going to live wonderful lives, there won't be any more nuclear bombs and cats will be fat, happy and fish-fed."

A dry note crept into Shower Curtain's wordless transmission. "You really believe that? I mean, would you use that as a basis for investing money in the stock market, or for starting a small business specializing in cat products that taste like fish?"

I played for time, licking at a kinked spot on my foreleg. "Well…"

Shower Curtain emitted a telepathic sigh. "Maybe you should just listen up and do what I tell you. Remember, I am a Being of Light."

I shrugged. "Yeah, okay." I let out a breath. "So spill it. What am I supposed to do?"

The right upper part of Shower Curtain's flowing presence moved, as if he had lifted a hand. "Don't laugh, now," he cautioned, "but here are the things you've got to create. It's a pretty long list."

Then, rather than explain through projected thoughts, he paraded more visions. He showed me seven rooms:

A "GAB ROOM" where people and cats got together and jabbered about whatever was on their minds. Doughnuts and sardines were served, hidden agendas were aired, people had heart-to-hearts, and everybody laughed a lot and high-fived.

A REFLECTION CHAMBER with the inside walls made of marbled-gold glass of the kind found in tacky casino resorts. Under the right conditions, you could see your reflection on the wall, which actually was like seeing your inner spirit and diagnosing all its flaws, which gave you a chance at perfection. But you couldn't see your reflection unless you had just lost 500 bucks shooting craps. So, not only could you see your reflection, you could see the reflection of your wife beating you over the head with her purse.

A MASSAGE CLINIC. Lots of purring and rubbing here, but no hanky-panky. World leaders were brought in to get their neck muscles caressed, easing their desire to get involved in internecine conflicts, brushfire wars and police actions.

A SENSORY-DEPRIVATION CHAMBER, in which people were deprived of all stimulation from MTV, video games, presidential press conferences and Oprah. Minds were cleared, sales of carbonated beverages went down, intelligence shot up.

A ROOM EQUIPPED with gadgets sold on late-night TV, such as the Salad Strewer and Poop-Heel's Pocket Fisherman.

These were used in tests of character. If a person used the device once and threw it away, her character was average. If she used it over and over and convinced herself she had gotten a bargain, she qualified for sainthood and psychiatric benefits.

AN AREA WHERE PEOPLE and cats could get psychic readings from people who spoke with Middle European accents and asked for the money up-front. This area was devoted to enlightenment: the enlightenment being that you don't get much for your money when you pay up-front.

A ROOM WITH A BED enhanced with musical components and Magic Fingers, which relaxed a person so deeply he thought the woman next to him was not his wife. Sometimes the relaxation was so deep that he could actually leave his body and hover above it. He was reluctant to do this, however, because he thought the woman next to him was not his wife.

When I had seen the visions, I was nonplussed. I also was a little upset. "How am I going to build these rooms?" I asked. "I don't know squat about spiritual things."

"Don't worry," intoned Shower Curtain. "You are destined to create these rooms to show people how to control their spiritual lives. Also, how to relax and get those kinks out of their backs that come from sitting too long hunched over. God will help you create these rooms. Whenever you need something, such as a small loan not to exceed $175, it will come to you."

I scratched at my chin. "Why me?"

"Because these things must be done on Earth by someone who is enlightened."

"Hey, pal, I may be enlightened, but I'm not on Earth, and I'm not going back."

"Actually, you are," said Shower Curtain and, with those words, my death came to an end.

Back for The Business

The demise ceremonies at the Special Cat Hospital weren't much. As Jed wept and turned away, Hans tossed a sheet of aluminum foil over my wilted body, transferred me to a chunk of pine board and handed me to Willi, who carted me down the hall.

I saw all this clearly because I'd been injected back through space and time to my perch in the air near the ceiling. As Willi stepped into the hall, I drifted along with him. He carried my body with one hand, took me into a storage room and dumped me on a steamer trunk to await disposal.

Then he left, and that would have written finis to my sordid life if it hadn't been for Jed. Good old faithful Jed. Here he came, blubbering and sad, stumbling into the storage room for a last good-bye. He hunched over me, his shoulders shaking. As he did, I was projected back into my body (Pain City!) and saw the aluminum foil above me gently pumping up and down, rattling faintly like a tin roof in a light breeze.

"He's breathing! He's alive!" Jed scrambled to the door to broadcast the news as I rotated out of my body, then in, then out. To their credit, here came Hans and Willi on the run, tumbling over themselves like crash-test dummies.

Hans reached me first, beefing out huge breaths. "He is alive, Mein Gott! But not for long if we don't get his liver quivering. Willi, crank up the electroshock!"

Hans was right. I was balancing on the narrow margin of life. I kept bouncing back into my body, feeling the throbbing of my bashed noggin and looking up at the uncooked-pizza faces of the vets, then flashing out again, flying back to the spot near the ceiling that gave me such a good view of the goings-on.

Now everything was a mad scramble. I floated above the tumult as Willi thundered down the hall toward the back of the hospital and Hans scooped me up and followed. Jed brought up the rear. We burst outdoors into a dusty, grass-tufted back yard. A wrecked Ford Taurus was there, its front fenders crushed in upon its tires, driver door open, hood up exposing the engine and battery. Jumper cables slithered from the battery terminals to two hamburger-patty cookers lying on a picnic blanket.

Down I went on the blanket, and Hans clapped the cookers to my scrawny chest. "Crank her, Willi," he bawled, and Willi pumped the starter of the Taurus, blasting the engine to life, sending a hell of a jolt through my meager chest and heart. And now I was really back inside my body, my fur snapping and sizzling, all my nerves whipping and popping, my tortured head pulsing like a hard-dribbled basketball.

World of Hurt

Let me tell you something: Once you get up into the nifty netherworld, once your address is a crystal garbage can, don't come back. Especially don't come back if what you're returning to is a body that has been belted with a tuna can, stuck full of Fizzy Cola, pummeled by a vet intent on vibrating your funny bone, and microwaved by two hamburger cookers attached to a Bammco Burp-Charge auto battery.

For a week after I returned to Earth, I lay prostrate, paralyzed, racked by Olympic-class suffering, a look on my face as if I was trying to ingest a tuba. I was a fright show for people from miles around, who trooped into the back room of the Special Cat Hospital to see the cat who had survived the trauma blitzkrieg. Upon seeing me, some hit the nausea button and gushered right on the floor. Whew! When you're hammered half to death, there's nothing like a little gastric juice to freshen up your room.

To get away from the scene, I'd sleep. And that was fantastic. Whenever I drifted off, I was back in those beautiful upper regions, all clean and airy, with Beings of Light teaching me new tricks. I'd thought my future visions were over, but no. I was shown supermarkets of the future, recycling bins of the future, newspapers of the future.

In the supermarkets of the future, products were still stamped with bar codes, but so were shoppers' foreheads. To choose among 26 kinds of cereal, shoppers would run their faces through a bar code reading device, then insert cereal boxes until one matched up with the shopper's personal preference brain bar code. There was no chance the shopper would pick Crunchfaster Malt-Grain Nuggets when his personal preference really ran to Coagulated Dates and Flattened Corn Kernels. The bar code made the choice. Instant happiness!

The recycling bins of the future were not for old newspapers, glass jars and plastic wrappers. They were for ideas. If your boss had an idea that didn't work, such as for restructuring the mail room, he'd toss it in the recycling bin. When he pulled it out a decade later, it still wouldn't work, but by then everybody would think it was brilliant because he'd quit and had been rehired as a consultant.

The newspapers of the future were especially cool. They were transmitted to hand-held devices, which were like two-way computer/radios linked to the newsrooms. Once you read a story, you could poke the headline and find out the real story by listening in on the reporters.

"What a bunch of foo-fer-aw that was," a reporter would say about a straight-faced story he'd written on the governor. "He's really taking that trade trip to China so he can get his secretary into a hotel room in Nanking and powder her earlobes."

"Yeah," a fellow reporter would rejoin. "And his wife is glad he's going because she's got a second mortgage on the house

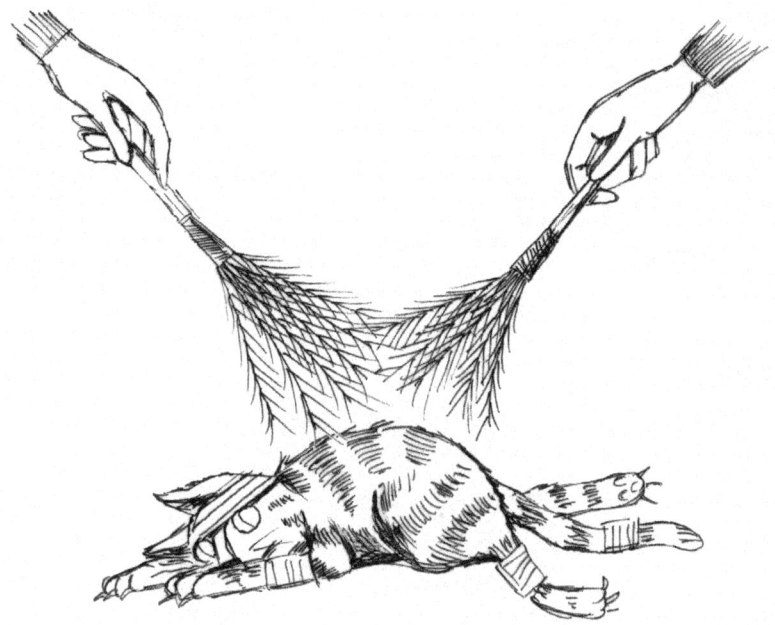

and invested the money in the opium trade. She hopes to take delivery on about 18 tons of product before he gets back. I'd hint at that in my column except that the paper needs the advertising from the auto-deodorizer businesses that are fronting her operation. Where will it all end?"

"Beats me," the first reporter would say. "Well, I've got to knock out a pretentious, misleading sidebar on the state's economy. See you."

As much fun as my sleeping moments were, my waking moments were grotesquely painful. I was alive, but I couldn't meow or even move my paws. Otherwise, I'd have clawed furrows into the backsides of the cat specialists from all over the country who were constantly coming to examine me.

One team of vets from New York couldn't believe I'd survived after being "dead" for so long, and they suspected my nervous system was abnormal. They devised a series of tests to see if they were right.

First, they tickled my ribs with feather dusters for 30 minutes at a time to see if I showed any reaction. It was awful. My whole body would swell and ripple with a giggle I couldn't let out. I felt like a balloon being blown up bigger and bigger but unable to burst. Laugh, cat, laugh, I ordered myself. But my body wouldn't obey.

In a second test, they sent mice dabbed with meat tenderizer scampering across my chest. They wanted to see if I'd involuntarily clutch at them. The saliva-flow from my mouth was like Niagara, but my synapses were in idle mode. My claws lay helplessly as I languished, hopelessly waiting for dinner. My nerves were shot.

Even though I'd supposedly come back from the dead, the doctors were convinced it was only a temporary reprieve. So were the nurses. So were my relatives. Two maiden aunt cats rode a baggage car all the way from St. Louis, traipsed in and checked me out for two minutes, then left for good.

"He looks like Jesus, doesn't he?" one said. "He's glowing like his ears are on fire."

"Hmmph," said the other one. "He looks like Jesus would if Jesus got his butt kicked by the welterweight contender. How come that lump on his head has eyes in it?"

"That *is* his head."

Thank goodness I could escape from all this by sleeping. In my dreams, the Beings of Light returned, issued explicit instructions on how to build the special rooms (cheery window treatment, plenty of electrical outlets) and gave me a deadline for finishing. I was more than willing to start, but my body wasn't responding.

Finally, after eight days, I was able to move a claw, then a paw, then my jaw. With tenacious and labored practice, some of my abilities gradually returned. I was able to roll over in bed. I could lick my fur in short sessions that wore me out. But on the nights Jed slept with me in the hospital, I still wasn't able to perform my catly duties, such as rambling across his chest or cutting off his airway by squatting on his face.

Nevertheless, after two weeks, Willi and Hans pronounced me ready to go home. And I did.

Bad Times

At home, Jed tucked me into a wicker basket on the terrace. I lay in the sun with dark swimming goggles to protect my eyes from the powerful glare, trying to work movement back into my limbs.

It was a long process. I'd still be overcome with weakness at the most inopportune times. Once when Jed brought me a saucer of milk, I bent down to take a drink and fell unconscious, my face plopping into the moo-juice. I would have drowned if Jed, who was returning to the house, hadn't glanced back and rushed to rescue me.

Most of the time I was alone in my basket, listening to the whirring of the cicadas in the paloverde trees, allowing myself to be lulled by the rat-tatting of Jed's computer keys from inside the casita as he banged out more and more greeting-card slogans to pay for the cost of getting me fixed up and rehabilitated.

I didn't mind the solitude. It gave me a chance to mull over the lessons the Beings of Light were teaching me. Each night when I fell asleep, and sometimes during my daytime naps, the Beings would conduct classes for me in how to build the special rooms that would save humankind from spiritual disaster and coffee nerves.

I was intrigued by the lessons, but the Beings didn't explain things well. In fact, they rarely explained them at all. Instead, they just ran through the motions of building the rooms and hoped I would get the hang of it. This was especially difficult because the Beings, who were short on manual dexterity, tended to hammer their thumbs instead of the nails. You want to know how an all-wise spiritual being reacts to a bludgeoned thumb? Sharply. Very sharply.

All the time I was working out my physical recovery, I was dealing with the experience I'd been through. When I blabbered about the Beings of Light and the crystal garbage cans and all, everyone thought I was crazy. Even Jed thought so, though he could see my new attitude wasn't just a mental aberration. It was built on solid changes. For one thing, he could see my communications skills were dramatically improved.

We had always been able to communicate pretty clearly in that non-verbal way used by many cats and their human friends. But this ability was terrifically enhanced by my trip up yonder. I could transmit thoughts to other people as well as Jed. It was as if I could actually speak to anyone, humans and animals alike. And did I communicate!

Whenever the mail carrier drifted by, she was treated to one of my talks about how the world was going to Hades if we all didn't cool out and start baking cookies. I was like a mad Christian cat, a latter-day feline version of John the Baptist, a meow crying in the desert, trying to make straight the ways of the bored.

It got so visitors stopped dropping by. Before, they had been able to enjoy a peaceful sojourn with Jed and me, engaging in a little delicate conversation, sipping iced sun tea, nibbling English water biscuits. Now the snacks were nowhere in evidence and they were assaulted by a freaked-out cat in black goggles ranting about future disasters and the need to build special rooms for everyone to flock into, regardless of fire codes and zoning restrictions.

Jed put up with my looniness, but I could see that he, too, was sad that the casita was now lonely all the time and that I seemed to be sinking deeper and deeper into my dementia, even as my physical abilities slowly returned. Finally, he took matters into his own hands. I found myself in a cat box in the deodorized back seat of Jed's Dodge Neon, headed for one of the most momentous meetings of my life.

I was on my way to meet Professor Bart Hogarth, who I later came to believe was the reincarnated spirit of Kwing Hao Po, a Second Century Chinese healer whose contacts with the spirit world have never been surpassed.

Hogarth's Lives

Instead of arranging an appointment with Professor Hogarth, Jed had chosen to have me visit one of the prof's classes at Cactus State University. We arrived shortly after the lecture had begun and Jed slipped me into a seat in the rear of the room. Then he walked out, leaving me to my own devices.

I wasn't sure what to expect. Hogarth, declaiming in a plucked-banjo voice, stalked back and forth in front of the class. He was an odd-looking specimen: broad-beamed, but with a narrow, dented head. His eyebrows were thin, mouth wide and quivering.

"The Near Death Experience changes somethin' in those it touches," he was asserting. "A personality that goes up the tunnel never slides back down the same." Hogarth pressed his large, soft hands together. "That's good, usually. If he does what those bein's up there tell him to do, that's good. Otherwise…"

Otherwise what? I began to ruminate on my own experience—the special rooms, the orders to build them. What would happen if I didn't come through? Would my world be utterly ruined?

Hogarth wasn't answering this question, and the students in their Gap jeans and Guess T-shirts didn't seem to care. They were massively bored, not even looking around to check out the room and the goggled-up, beaten-down cat in the rear.

"…anyone who has, I'd surely like to know," Hogarth droned on. "Trackin' down research subjects isn't easy. So let me say it again, if any of you-all have the acquaintance of any soul who's had a Near Death encounter, I'd appreciate it if you'd pass that name on to me."

Suddenly my paw was in the air. "I have!" I exclaimed, "I've just had one." I heard myself burbling, my voice cracking somewhere between a maniacal laugh and a scream. "I can't stand it any longer! It's blown my fur backwards."

Now I'd gotten their attention. Wide, cow-like eyes turned toward me, mouths hung slack, fingernails paused in the act of scratching scrawny chests. One girl with sinuous brown hair caught sight of me for the first time and gasped.

Hogarth was self-possessed. He harrumphed once, marched to me. "Get a grip," he ordered, placing a doughy hand on one of my narrow shoulders. I could feel an intense warmness in his palm, a transfer of energy that swept through me, soothing my blood. "I've been down this road before. Just you calm yourself and we'll deal with it."

My voice caught in my throat. "Dying isn't easy," I quavered.

Hogarth's face was close to mine, a crooked grin jagging his odd mouth. "Oh, you're wrong about that," he said. "As any actor will tell you, dying IS easy. It's comedy that's hard."

Rocking Chairs

Professor Bart Hogarth has been described as a combination of Mr. Wizard and Yogi Bear. On the one hand, he's so smart that he can set up and operate any brand of DVR without even looking at the instruction book. On the other hand, he sometimes responds to the most serious lines of argument by letting his lower lip droop, crossing his eyes and blurting, "Yabba-dabba-do!"

I was treated immediately to his odd sense of humor when he pulled up to Jed's casita the day after I visited his class. He was driving a six-year-old minivan splashed with finger-painted astrological symbols, a sly jape on those who considered him a cuckoo.

When he entered the living room, we formed an immediate bond. Because of my limited mobility, I hadn't been able to exercise as I fought my way back to health, so Jed had gotten me a rocking chair, which let me get the sensation of movement just by shifting my haunches. In fact, Jed had gotten me several rocking chairs. An antique store, which was closing, had offered a package deal on half-a-dozen chairs, and Jed thought different styles would tickle my imagination and keep me rocking.

Hogarth loved my collection of chairs. He told me that some of his most productive ideas wafted into his brain while he rocked slowly for hours, his eyes half-closed, his belly full of pumpkin pie. Soon we were facing each other, rocking away and talking up a storm.

Actually, I did most of the talking. After blabbering on and on about my Near Death Experiences to people who didn't understand, I was frustrated. Now that I had found a man who believed in this stuff, who took it seriously, I couldn't control myself. I let everything out in a rush: my horrible accident, the wild ride into a Heaven complete with animated shower curtains and television stomachs, and my visions of the future.

Hogarth showed little emotion. That bugged me. He asked questions in a flat voice, didn't change expression, didn't lead me or encourage me. But I soon learned it wasn't for lack of interest. He simply didn't want to influence me, to inadvertently give me information that would lead me to embellish. He was a true scientist: objective, calm, pie-fed.

At first, I contented myself with telling him about my journey and didn't bother him with my anxieties. I was afraid if I got too emotional he might think I was a psycho. As I talked, I felt a new self-assurance. Perhaps I had changed.

"As you know," I said, "there are realms beyond our day-to-day world. Marvelous places where all is peaceful and pleasant. However, I never knew these places were peopled by bathroom furnishings."

Dr. Hogarth chewed his lower lip. "You are referring, of course, to the spirit guide you know as Shower Curtain."

"I am."

"Tell me," said Hogarth. "Did this being move freely, or was it pulled along a shower rod by those little clip-together thingies?"

"On its own," I replied. "And it seemed to have Wisdom."

Hogarth rocked and thought. "Well, Wisdom sometimes resides in the humblest things," he said. "For instance, soap dishes have given me some pretty good tips on the horses. Also, toothbrush holders."

"Really?"

He smiled. "No, not really. I scrutinize the Racing Form, just like everybody else. I was just testing you to see if you were gullible."

"And am I gullible?"

"Oh, boy."

I can't say I was pleased by this reaction, but, still, he was being honest.

I sighed and tongued some errant fur back into place on my right forepaw. "So what should I do now?"

"What do YOU think you should do?"

"Oh, no," I said. "You aren't one of those non-directional therapists, are you?"

Hogarth smiled broadly. "I am. It's much less work. And, frankly, that Freudian stuff is just so much cat poo."

Hmm. So he wasn't going to be any help. Well, I guessed that was the point. You paid more for no help than for help–sort of like the way restaurants used to serve you free water, then put it in a fancy bottle and made it more expensive than beer.

I tried out a possibility: "Well, I think I need to build the Gizmos of Salvation."

"Makes sense to me," said Hogarth. Perhaps he WAS just being non-directional, but suddenly his rocking speeded up; the porch boards creaked, and I felt a surge of energy. There was a tickle somewhere inside my fur, and I was vibrating with excitement. Could one cat save the world? Maybe yes, maybe no. If I could, though, I would certainly earn a lifetime supply of fish sticks.

In A Glass Darkly

I decided to start with the Reflection Chamber. Don't ask me why. I've always been wary of mirrors. I once scared the feces out of myself by walking in front of a highly polished coffeepot that had been placed on the floor so the maid could clean a countertop. When I saw a vicious cat with a don't-mess-with-me face, I jumped two feet in the air and landed, hissing, in a karate stance. The maid threw a rag at me and startled me back to reality.

Now, however, the Reflection Chamber obsession was upon me, and I fell to with a vengeance. As it turned out, an abandoned motel a half-mile from Jed's casita was packed with enough mirrors to populate the Palace of Versailles. There were mirrors in the bathrooms, mirrors in the bedrooms, even mirrors across from the check-in desk so the clerk could see if firearms were sticking out of guests' back pockets.

I didn't bother to ask Jed to find the owners. I just employed a couple of stew-bums from the local watering hole to loot the place and bring the haul to me, telling Jed I intended to build a Native American sweat lodge in the back yard. He readily agreed, thinking the labor would draw me out of my funk.

Things went quickly. I got the walls up in a week—plywood panels braced with two-by-fours—and threw a tarp over the hole in the top. Some light leaked through. To supplement that illumination, I ran a 12-socket electrical extension cord from an outlet on Jed's back porch and plugged in a jumble of other cords ending in reflectorized electric bulbs. It was a thing of beauty: curving, looping cords, pools of artificial light, mirrors throwing back dark, pullulating images. I plopped a ratty sofa in the middle of the room so visitors could relax as they sent their minds soaring into the deep reflections on the walls.

Hogarth was fascinated. "So, you think you'll be able to see spirits in there? Really?"

I couldn't tell if he was serious, though he seemed so. He certainly had that long-faced look.

"Yes," I told him. "This will be like Wisdom on Steroids. In peering into these mirrors, people will see deep into their own souls, into the souls of all humanity. They'll be able to ferret out the glitches that keep them from being happy."

He shook his head. "There's a whole lot of detritus in a soul, you know. A soul is kind of like an enclosed back porch where you throw everything you don't need. Be careful that your vision isn't clogged up by old washing machines, cast-off dog dishes, and pieces of carpet left over from re-doing the bedroom."

Did this warning bother me? Well, a little. But I wasn't going to be put off. I decided to try the Reflection Chamber full-bore just as the sun set on Friday. I considered inviting Jed to join me, but I was afraid the experience would worry him. These days, he tip-toed around me, giving me supportive looks that told me he sure hoped I could work things out. No, for this adventure, I needed Hogarth.

The good doctor showed up on time, just as the sun was sinking behind the saguaros and the red light was dying on the Sierra Estrella. The shadows were reaching out to us from the scrub brush and the greasewood trees, and small creatures were scurrying off to places of rest. Hogarth was dressed for the occasion. He'd salvaged a suit from Goodwill, dyed it inky black and festooned the inside with Brooks Brothers labels.

We stood for a moment in the growing darkness—the inquisitive scientist and the cat on a world-saving mission—then creaked back the makeshift door and plunged into a world beyond imagination.

I'd left the extension bulbs off, so the interior seemed to float and shimmer with a strange liquid-y mix of shadow and leaked-in evening light. As we moved, our images—first large, then thin, then wavy and weird—vibrated on the walls. It was dark. The bulbs on the extension cords awaited the twitch of a switch. Hogarth and I tiptoed over the sandy earth floor of the chamber (I had decided to save money by leaving this part au naturel) and plopped onto the discarded sofa.

I shuffled my haunches on the cushions, feeling uneasy. On a small table next to the sofa, I had placed a pitcher of Kool-Aid and two glasses. Perhaps a big slug of Kool-Aid would calm my nerves. I reached for the pitcher, but in the darkness, I plunged my paw into the liquid. Ewww! I flipped the paw repeatedly, trying to dry it.

The darkness deepened. The reflected images seemed to grow and swell and enfold us. I imagined ancient Roman warriors rising from the ground, Native American witch doctors coalescing around me, monstrous Pakistani fortune tellers nodding and mumbling. My stomach felt cold. My muscles vibrated. It was too dark, too dark. I wanted to paw the electric switch near me, to sweep away these shadows!

Hogarth's restraining hand calmed me. The shadows continued to grow, but now the reflections were coming out to me, pulling me in. I was walking through the walls, proceeding outward into infinite space. I started looking around for insights, for answers to the deepest human questions, for visions of interior reality. All I could see below me, though, was a pile of beer cans, pop bottles, and pizza boxes. Apparently, I was drifting over a dump.

Things were going terribly wrong. Was I sleepwalking? Had I somehow escaped the surly bonds of the Reflection Chamber, only to be punished with sights of mundane reality? I stretched out my forepaw, trying to hit the electric switch and throw some light on this subject. Too late, I realized I was reaching with my wet paw.

A sizzling pain shot through me; I could feel my fur sparking and popping. I convulsed and arched my back, trying to escape the surge of electricity. Could nothing save me? I was in torment. Then my brain snapped off.

I was drifting through space again. I looked down, trying to locate the dump, but it wasn't there. Everything below was crystal, and my surroundings were all quiet and peaceful and dark. And profound. I looked to my right. Yes, there was Shower Curtain.

"You never learn, do you?" he said.

Open Ticket

"A repeat customer!" exulted Willi. "And one that's been twice to The Suburb Beyond the Suburb. Don't see this every day."

The beast I was looking down on, stretched at length on a poker table in the Special Cat Hospital, was singed beyond belief. That was me, but I barely recognized my body. My fur was all fricasseed, and I had a dark mark on my right forepaw where the electricity had shivered through the moisture and lit me up.

Oddly, though, I realized the damage was mostly cosmetic. Death had whisked me away and plopped me down again, but without wrecking my body. In a microsecond, I had been scooped beyond the Veil without all that nonsense about boiling my blood, short-circuiting my brain, and snuffing my breath.

I realized that my first death experience had set me up for an easy passage to the Other Side. Whenever the Deity left the door ajar—in this case, via blasting me with 120 volts of electricity—I could be jerked through without getting my carcass ravaged. As I had this thought, I realized it came from infused knowledge. Death had given me ultimate insight. Cool. I sat up.

"What the hell!" exclaimed Hans. "I didn't even get a chance to try the Fizzy Cola!" He was pale and shaking—I could see the blubber rolling like waves beneath his tie-dyed muscle shirt—and he almost dropped the bottle of pop. To steady himself, he took a long swig, and the carbonation welled out of his lips and dribbled down his front.

Willi was equally nonplussed. "All of a sudden, there's something not very dead about this cat!" he whispered, and looked over at Jed and Dr. Hogarth, who were watching the spectacle. Jed was wet-eyed and worried, but Hogarth's expression was distant, as if he had been composing a few paragraphs for an article on the Phenomenon of the Near Death Cat.

I shook myself all over, and burnt fur flew like cotton fluff. "Let's get out of here," I said. "I'm probably going to need a little Petroleum Jelly to soothe this poached paw, but other than that I'm right as rain."

So off we went. I didn't explain much on the way home, except to let on that I was now apparently a resident of both the physical world and the spirit world, able to move back and forth quite easily, as long as someone helped me out a little bit by setting off a 10-megaton bomb in my litter box just as I was doing my business. Yeah, yeah, it felt good, conquering Death, and knowing I had done it.

I slept well that night, woke up and ate a big breakfast. I had a saucer of milk, two fish heads and a little chunk of filet, medium-rare, finished off with catnip. I still smelled like a mink coat with smoke damage, but I felt fine. Even the mark on my paw had faded to a small welt.

I expected Hogarth to be ooh-ing and aah-ing as we resumed our session in the rocking chairs, but he didn't seem impressed.

"You had yourself quite an experience there," he said. He was smoking a corn-cob pipe, like a character in a hillbilly cartoon. "Quite an experience. I suppose you think you're somethin' special."

"Well…yeah," I said. "I mean, I *am* something special. One of a kind. Jed used to leave his *Collected Shakespeare* on the floor, so I read *Hamlet*. How about that? Death is 'that undiscovered country, from whose bourne no traveler returns.' And remember what Paul Newman said in *Hud*, you know, that movie where Patricia Neal is an unlikely target for erotic urges? Hud says, 'Nobody gets out of life alive.' That about sums it up, doesn't it?"

Hogarth allowed a long breath of smoke to issue into the cool morning air, and looked a long way out over the desert. "Well, technically, you didn't get out of life alive. You died and came back. Quickly, of course, but there was a definite transition."

"So?"

He gestured with the pipe. "All I am sayin' is that what goes up doesn't necessarily come down. You've got it in your head that you can just bang back and forth between the physical realm and the Great Beyond whenever it suits you. Like you are some kind of Spirit Traveler with a train schedule tucked behind your ear and a change of fur in your overnight bag. Not so."

I was miffed. "Say, who's got the infused knowledge here, anyway?" I said. "I'm the one who went to the Other Side and brought back insights. I know what's what. You are just a hick Arizonan with a fake Southern accent. You claim to know a lot, but what do you really know? You don't even have a Spirit Guide!"

He smiled easily, unruffled. "True," he said. "I get *my* Shower Curtain at Bed, Bath and Beyond. But I least I know what it costs. And I also know that it's made in China."

The Sparks Fly Upward

So, my first attempt to build one of the Gizmos of Salvation hadn't worked. So what? I was determined to go on, to show Hogarth that I could pull off something like this and, yes, to save humanity. It's true that saving humanity had dropped way down my list of priorities, but it still was on there. I still had a mission, damn it, even if everybody thought I was an ego monster.

Hogarth was off somewhere buying mango yogurt and asparagus, so I explained my next plan to Jed. We used the living room. Jed sat in an overstuffed chair done in paisley-patterned Naugahyde. I paced about on the parquet, occasionally soothing my tootsies on the Navajo rug. Jed even took notes on a legal pad. I know he meant to show he was interested in my thoughts. More likely, he was just jotting down greeting-card slogans.

"How about I build the Massage Room?" I said. "I could pull the mirrors out of the Reflection Chamber, have an electrician redo the wiring, and cover the floor with Persian carpets made in Taiwan. Then we could hire the girls from Maisie's Kitty-Cat down the street to come in and palpate the neck muscles of whatever world leaders we can attract. That would calm them down. They would lazily wave away any suggestions that they blow each other to smithereens in an effort to secure world domination."

Jed half-smiled and wrote something.

"You sure that was a note on the Massage Room?" I asked suspiciously. "Or was it a humorous line for people celebrating St. Swithin's Day?"

Jed half-smiled again and clutched the legal pad closer to his chest.

"Okay, sure," I said, and dropped the subject. "We'll need to get the newspaper reporters out here. Whenever there's a world conclave, that's how people learn about it. Besides, we're short on money to send telegrams, and e-mails to Bora Bora and Waziristan would just get spammed out."

So that was what we did. The reporters descended, the stories went out, and things worked like a charm. It must have been a slow week for world conclaves. Or maybe wherever these potentates were from, the weather was crappy, so they all decided a couple of days in El Macho would be just the thing. Either that, or…well, Maisie's did advertise a World Famous Massage. I always thought that was hype. Maybe not.

At any rate, two weeks later, the empty field next to Jed's casita was filled with helicopters emblazoned with the insignias of 78 different countries, principalities and caliphates. The dress was varied and colorful. Yes, there were lots of three-piece suits, but there were also robes, burnooses, headdresses, turbans, kilts and a fez or two.

The Massage Room was tricked out with patchouli oil burners, soft lights and wall hangings featuring scenes from the Kama Sutra in graffiti spray-painted by a West Side gangbanger. Unfortunately, the banger didn't realize the Kama Sutra was a sensuous Indian epic: He believed it was some kind of supercharged, modified Pontiac. Because of that, the scenes featured a plethora of chain-link steering wheels, wind scoops and underslung rear ends. Even so, the effect was surprisingly captivating.

Hogarth shook his head at all this, but what did he know? Despite his doubts, he agreed to host the proceedings. I was busy with the final arrangements, and I wanted to be the star of the show, after all, not some functionary with a microphone in my hand working up the crowd.

There were too many guests to fit in the Massage Room, of course, so we set up a huge outdoor area replete with folding chairs from the local American Legion hall. Our makeshift stage was the flatbed of an empty semi-trailer truck "borrowed" from a customer at a nearby diner. I told the waitress to flirt with the trucker and keep refilling his coffee: By the time his kidneys protested, our stage show would be over and we would have ensured a peaceful future.

Hogarth warmed up the crowd by telling a few jokes and smacking his lips over the wonders of the Massage Room. He underemphasized the spiritual enlightenment to be gained from a neck massage, but I aimed to correct that. I didn't have long to wait.

"And h-e-e-re's Dun-DEE!" Hogarth proclaimed.

I sashayed out to thunderous applause. As I began my pitch, everyone seemed to be in a good mood. That didn't last.

"You people are DOOMED!" I shouted, spreading my paws wide. "You have been EVIL and you need to REPENT!"

The crowd muttered. Attendees shifted their feet, and I heard hundreds of folding chairs creak. I could sense their anger building. I hoped that Security had checked everyone for firearms, but I realized that was unlikely. For one thing, this was Arizona. For another thing, there was no Security. We had been too rushed to hire any.

At my elbow, Hogarth tried to slow me down. "Let's not be *castigatin'* these folks, now," he said under his breath. "You're supposed to be bringin' a message of peace and *hope*."

"I'm going to save these bozos by telling them the TRUTH," I whispered back. "I'm the one who knows the ultimate reality. I'VE BEEN THERE!"

I turned back to the crowd.

"You are all SWINE," I cried. "Your future is HORRIBLE unless you start getting along. Do you think you can save yourselves by getting your neck manipulated? Do you really think a hot towel over your face and a shoulder massage— however much it makes your muscles melt and induces a drowsy feeling that could lead to a really good nap—can keep the world from ULTIMATE DESTRUCTION?" I paused for the big finish. "GOD CHUCKLES IN YOUR FACE!"

More muttering. I belatedly realized that many of these visitors probably were armed, and that they might take my gentle efforts to save them as insults. Hmmm. I needed to re-think this.

About this time, I saw the sun flash off something far back in the crowd. At first, I thought it was a pocket mirror. Then, I realized it was a telescopic sight. In such a situation, your mind denies reality: When I heard the KA-POW, I thought a truck tire had blown out on the Interstate.

I believed that for a full microsecond. Then the high velocity bullet redecorated my chest, stifled my glottis and sent my vital organs on a long vacation. I didn't feel any of this, though. Apparently my passage off this mortal coil was getting to be pretty much painless. In an instant, I was detached from the earth, floating, floating, floating. Three lives down, six to go.

Road Trip

There was barely a dent in my chest. Hans poked it with a grubby finger. "They ain't making high-powered rifles the way they used to, is all I can say. This wound, if you can call it that, looks more like somebody removed a pimple with a rusty spoon."

I was lying on the examining table, completely awake and more than a little miffed. "Yeah, well then, why am I here?"

Willi piped up. "Because your friend saw your torso flying in 40 different directions and thought you might require an adhesive bandage. Or maybe 40 adhesive bandages. He didn't figure you would reassemble so nice on your own."

"Hogarth?"

The fat vet shook his head and jabbed a thumb over his right shoulder. Jed.

I sat up and looked my owner full in the face. "So Hogarth took a runner, did he?" I said. "When this Saving Humanity thing gets a little problematical, he beats feet back to the lab and leaves me twisting slowly, slowly in the wind."

"It's not like that at all," said Jed. "He's out there trying to convince the authorities that this is a case for Homicide and not for Animal Control. Furthermore, he's shopping for mango yogurt and asparagus so you can have a nice dinner. He knows your importance to the Future, but nobody else is willing to admit it."

Well, that's it, I thought to myself, *How much can one cat do?* Jed did what he could to cheer me up. He took me out for brunch at Pancake Alley, a Tex-Mex waffle establishment that welcomes personal pets, and bought me a plate of Italian sausages. It wasn't enough to mollify me. I was formulating a plan, and as soon as I got back to the casita, I put it into practice.

"I'm hitting the road," I told Jed. "I'm going on the bum. Clearly my efforts to use the special knowledge I have gained have come to nothing. When Hogarth gets back, tell him the Noble Experiment is finished."

I thought about bundling up a few of my cat toys and packing a tuna lunch, but my dreadful life experience (or life-and-death experience) had begun with errant tuna. I realized munching more of it might bring on Post-Traumatic Cat Syndrome, so I forgot about that. Jed was so stunned that he said nothing as I pranced out. I suppose he just thought, "Well, he'll be out all night, but he'll come back in the morning." People take cats for granted like that, even cats with special powers.

Midafternoon found me in Texas, or at least I took it to be Texas. I'd ambled down to a truck stop, curled up among a load of tires on a parked semi, and dropped off to sleep. By the time I awakened, the semi was parked outside a coffee-taco-and-egg emporium on a stretch of highway that seemed as bleak as Arizona, but dustier. Ergo, Texas. I hopped down, figuring I would stretch my legs for the next few miles.

It wasn't hot—not all *that* hot, anyway. And there was no wind. The desert was like all flatland in the western United States. Hard, spiny plants, sandy earth, lots of scuttling creatures. And lonely. I didn't expect to find company along the highway, but I topped a rise about an hour after I left the truck and there was an Irish setter trundling along. He looked harmless enough. His head was down and his hindquarters were humping like a half-flat car tire.

I caught up with him, but he barely looked around. After a while he spoke, though. I wasn't surprised. I had begun to accept the fact that I could communicate with animals and humans as if we were all batting the breeze at a coffee klatch. "You've got a unique air about you," Woofer said. "You've got that cat thing going on, of course, that hot-stuff attitude, usually undeserved. But you also carry yourself with melancholy pride, almost doom-laden, as if you had seen the future of all living things and had been unhappily surprised."

"Funny you should say that," I replied. "As it turns out, I've been killed three times and come back, so my omniscience is up to snuff. I can't get my message across, though. The world is an ignorant place, full of people who don't appreciate good literature, who espouse provincial ideas, who ignore the heart-healthy diet items on the menu and refuse to attend any movies with subtitles. I am a cat crying in the wilderness, 'Make straight the ways of the Lord.' If there were a Lord, I mean. And ways."

"I hear you," said Woofer. "By the way, my name is Woofer."

"Dundee Blinky," I replied. "I was already calling you Woofer in my mind. It's nice to have an absurd experience that meets expectations."

We walked along, totally comfortable. Now there was a slight breeze, and the sound of birdsong from the creosote bush. "Are you, by any chance, some kind of spiritual guide for me? I'm getting used to that happening."

"I'm a hound dog," Woofer said. "There's nothing special about me. Keep in mind that you can learn things from the most mundane experiences and the most ordinary companions. Perhaps you are familiar with the Zen of the Householder? Paying full attention to the simplicities of housekeeping? Things don't have to be high-falutin' to give you insights."

"I suppose not," I said, somewhat disappointed. "But we always need to be going forward, don't we? I mean, we get so caught up in the day-to-day routine that we aren't alert to the mystical dimensions of life. We don't tap into the unspoken wisdom of those around us, or reach vital accommodation with the cosmos."

"Sometimes life is just life; we need to accept that," said Woofer. "There's nothing wrong with the day-to-day routine. We aren't angels or demons. We are just us. It's good enough just to eat, sleep, and keep an eye out for speeding Pontiacs."

"I get your point about the routine," I said. "But I'm not sure I understand your reference to Pontiacs."

"Look over your shoulder," he replied.

I did, but it was too late.

A Metaphor
I Didn't Like

The thing was, I was NOT floating through space, I was NOT communing with Shower Curtain. After the gunshot had splattered my torso, I'd had only a brief experience of that. Still, I'd had some. That here-we-go-again feeling had assured me I was having another la-la Near Death Experience and not venturing into the Infinite Void without a return booking.

I'd missed that on this go-round. It's true, though, that I was not hurting. But I apparently was also not a candidate for Miss Paws of Midland, Texas. Which is to say, if my metaphors are too obtuse, that I wasn't pretty. I heard Woofer bleating out concerned barks, and what sounded like cheeping from a heron with stomach distress. I opened my eyes. Woofer, check. Heron, no check. A roadrunner had joined our merry little band, and was commiserating with the canine.

Now they ceased making sub-human sounds and returned to using human speech. How convenient for you, the reader.

Woofer held the floor (actually, the roadside), and he was explaining things to the roadrunner. "We were just ambling along, having a conversation," he said, "We had just begun discussing the relative merits of cosmic profundity versus matter-of-fact acceptance of life, and THIS happened."

The bird sniffed. "No exploration of anthroposophy?" he asked. "I hope not. It's illogical. Absurd, really."

"No, no," protested Woofer. "Just the usual chit-chat you might expect when a cat meets a dog out in the middle of nowhere. Oh, hey, look, he's awake."

I didn't bother to get up, not just yet. "What are you pulling?" I said to Woofer. "You knew that Pontiac was coming and allowed me to stray right in front of it. Now I look like hell, don't I? I look like hell!"

The roadrunner was the one who answered. "Yes, superficially you appear to have lost a chain-saw fight. To judge from your ability to speak, however, that's more an optical illusion than anything. Yes, yes, now I see. You are already healing…healing…and now you are perfect again!"

I stood up, shook some turn-light shards out of my fur, and adopted an indignant expression. "You two are agents of the afterlife, are you not?" I said. "It can't be a coincidence that I keep cycling over to the other side and then back. I've changed into a creature with ambiguous mortality. Obviously, whoever has changed me needs to keep an eye on me. That's why you two are here."

The roadrunner made a clicking sound with his beak. "I don't think so. We are just the typical animal companions who befriend you, accompany you part way on your journey, offer sage bits of wisdom, then disappear, leaving you to your own devices. You have overwritten our parts."

I decided to test him. "So, then, how long is my journey?"

"The span of a day."

"And how long is that day?"

"As long as you make it."

I pawed my forehead. "So you are saying that our life can seem long or short, depending on how we approach it?"

"Well, I didn't say that exactly, but that's catchy. I like that."

"I suppose your name is Beep-Beep. That's what roadrunners always say in cartoons."

"No," he replied. "My name is actually Alphonse de la Cognac, Third Count of Monserrat."

"I think I'll call you Beep-Beep."

"Sure, that's fine."

I tested all my parts to make sure everything was working. Woofer tried out his hindquarters, bouncing them up and down like a kid trying out the springs in a busted sofa. Beep-Beep made little dashes here and there, warming up his engine.

Our conversation seemed to be over, but I couldn't let it go. My surroundings seemed real enough, but I had to be sure.

"Is Texas a metaphor for something?" I asked.

"Yes," said Beep-Beep. "For hot emptiness, long highways, and dead armadillos. Shelter is far away, and this looks like it is going to be a long day. A real one, not a metaphorical construct."

"Given that," said Woofer, "shouldn't we be going?"

The Funny Farm

It was a long afternoon. I found out that there is nothing so endless as a Texas highway. Still, Woofer and Beep-Beep were good company. We revisited my experiences in life, with particular emphasis on my fatalities and their aftermaths. They had questions about Jed, and especially about Hogarth.

"Is he as charismatic as they say?" Woofer asked me. "I've been told that he can really light up a room."

I thought about the professor and was sorry I hadn't said goodbye to him. "Yes, his personality certainly has plenty of throw weight," I replied. "Still, there's a gentleness to him that no-one much talks about. When you are selecting an adviser on the Great Beyond, you want someone with a warm bedside manner, or at least I do."

Beep-Beep, always the skeptic, piped up with his usual malarkey: "Yes, you liked him so well that you gave him the go-bye while he was out shopping for mango yogurt and asparagus. That's one meal you will never enjoy."

"If by that you mean I will never again be able to take advantage of his wisdom, I beg to differ. It's just that I need to get out and find things out for myself. I have a lot to offer, too, you know."

"Speaking purely as a roadrunner, I'm not sure about that," Beep-Beep returned. "There's a lot of ego in your makeup, and it doesn't seem that getting killed four times has changed that."

"This isn't just about me," I said with irritation. "The lessons I am learning can be applied to humanity in general and to animal-ity in general, too!"

"Exactly what I mean," replied Beep-Beep. "You are a blowhard and a know-it-all, not to say a narcissist, and that approach is leading you astray. You have been given the opportunity to explore the secrets of the universe, and all you think of is what a big deal you are."

Fortunately, Woofer stepped in to calm things down with his well-grounded hound dog approach. "Now, now," he said. "We are all pilgrims on this journey. The fact that we go looking for truth doesn't diminish the flaws in our personalities. We must try to find truth despite our shortcomings. Dundee is no less a truth seeker just because he is, as you have pointed out, a world-class gasbag."

That made me feel a lot better. Woofer had really stuck it to Beep-Beep.

I think.

We proceeded on our way, past Jointed Goatgrass, Itchgrass and Western Bitterweed, not to mention Dwarf Glasswort, Bushy Bluestem and Pricky Ash. I thought I noted some unusual creatures, too: the Hispid Cotton Rat, the American Wigeon, the Red-Eared Slider and the Keeled Earless Lizard. But perhaps I was mixing up my flora and fauna from all over Texas. Close observation has never been my strong point.

A couple of hours later, we had walked several miles. The desert descended into a flat valley with a ridgeline beyond and, in the middle distance, a meandering river. Grass and trees huddled along the watercourse. In the middle of the greenery, I saw a group of buildings.

"Oh, here we are, the Funny Farm," said Beep-Beep. I thought I detected a dark premonition in his tone.

As we came closer, I noticed cats running here and there. Actually, I would have said they were cavorting, or capering, or frolicking. Or possibly gamboling, romping, or carousing. We proceeded down a long driveway and entered a central yard. At one end stood a pint-sized Quonset Hut with a sign over the entrance: "Administration." I followed Woofer and Beep-Beep inside. A cat in a flat-topped U.S. Marines ball cap—cat size—lounged behind a small desk.

"Room for the night?" he asked, pushing across a clipboard with a pen attached. With surprising skill, Beep-Beep caught up the pen with one foot and scrawled something on the board. The clerk looked at us narrowly. "Building No. 8," he said. "We're running low on catnip. The boys have been acting up, so you'll have to find your own fun. And if you want a snack, you'll have to make do with whatever small rodents you can hunt."

"Don't worry about us," Woofer replied. "We are hardy travelers on the road of life, and we have come to the Funny Farm simply to assure ourselves that the mysteries of life can't be found in chemical substances. That they, in fact, lead to feline degradation."

"You can say that again," the clerk replied. "Like I say, the boys have been acting up."

We made our way to Building No. 8. The shadows of the trees lengthened before us. Evening was coming on.

We entered the barracks-like building. Already, though it was not yet nightfall, we could hear drunken snoring coming from several bunks. In the center of the room, four cats were playing poker, or trying to. They kept fumbling the cards and dropping them, and laughing uproariously. Another cat lay on the floor retching.

"The effects of catnip," Woofer asserted.

I protested. "But catnip is simply a perennial herb of the mint family that causes temporary ecstasy in cats. Surely these reactions are excessive."

"Not here," Woofer said. "Not at the Funny Farm. Here the cats dissolve it and drink it, smoke it, huff it, and snort it. They have it in their heads that catnip will remove their inhibitions and allow them to gain personal insights, that excess will lead to knowledge. Well, you see the true effects. Beware."

He looked around. "I suppose we should settle in."

A Breath of No Air

It was a cold night. In the Texas hinterlands at this time of year, the temperature plunges once the sun goes down. When darkness descended in the barracks and the caterwauling cats subsided, we all found places to sleep. Woofer and Beep-Beep chose a couple of the empty bunks, but I wanted to get away from the rabble. I had some thinking to do, and I couldn't do it amid all the snoring and rustling and sleep-talking.

I found myself a small room off the main living area. Really, it was more like a storage closet. But at least there were a couple of blankets in there and, miracle of miracles, a propane heater. I was going to be plenty toasty tonight, while all those other catnip-addled felines shivered.

I fired up the heater. The device kicked out enough warmth to do the job, and I increased the effect by closing the closet door. Ideal! I drifted off to sleep meditating on the significance of all the experiences I'd had. The Fatal Tuna. The Electric

Kool-Aid Acid Test. The Assassin's Bullet. The Pontiac of Death. And, mixed in with all these fatal encounters, the lessons I had been exposed to. For instance, that crystal was a favored decorative motif in heaven. That you could see your ancestors and everybody else's ancestors in a mirror if you sat real still, but that it wasn't wise to overload an electric socket. That people with guns didn't like having their motives questioned. That speeding automobiles didn't pay much attention to what was in their way.

And beyond that, on a more ethereal level, that it was easy to confuse your feelings of righteousness with actually being righteous. That you shouldn't turn your back on your friends when things don't work out. That you may think you have a great message for the world, but that message may not benefit you: In other words, the cat who brings the pizza doesn't necessarily get to eat it. And, oh yeah, don't do drugs. Or catnip.

With these ruminations rolling about, I nestled down. I awoke in the middle of the night experiencing an array of unpleasant symptoms: headache, dizziness, nausea, chest pain and confusion. I managed to stagger out of my blankets and over to the closed door. I pushed it open, but I had used the last of my strength. I collapsed.

Or did I? I seemed to be outside now, with the night sounds around me and the smell of Smart Swampweed and Marsh Fleabane in the air. I felt physically good now, and everything was quiet as I walked along. It didn't even seem to be cold. I was lighter than air.

The night was friendly, and my mind was working overtime. For some reason, I was envisioning a headline I'd once seen: CAT KILLED BY CARBON MONOXIDE FROM PROPANE HEATER. Where had I read that? With my mind's eye, I looked at the newspaper again. It was the front page of the *Dallas Morning News*, and this was a banner headline. The date was tomorrow!

With a sinking feeling, I realized that tomorrow would be a slow news day.

Loss Leader

That news article was a turning point for me. It was not only a slow news day but a slow week for the *Dallas Morning News*, so the reporter who handled the story was sent out to do an in-depth yarn about my background. And he came up with the whole sordid tale: all the deaths due to tuna can, electrocution, shooting, car crash, asphyxiation. I became known as a survivor, the kind of character admired by the American public, and as a mystic who had wandered in the spirit world.

I drifted about through the South, the Midwest, the Northeast, the Southeast, all over. Wherever I went, I earned a few bucks telling my story. Usually I was a big hit. Not so much in Omaha, though. I rented a hall downtown and talked about the beauty of the Higher Realms. There's beauty on the Other Side, I told the audience. But don't go there right away. There's always something to live for, even if the University of Nebraska Cornhuskers have a losing football season. That statement raised some eyebrows. Those in attendance wanted me gone.

They threw a few dollars at me and turned their backs, and I was on my way.

My adventures continued. In the Ozarks, I parlayed my public-speaking gig into a job as minister of a church, but had to leave when the congregation tried to pay me in methamphetamine.

In Paducah, Kentucky, I ran a financial advice firm, telling people to "lay up treasures for yourself in heaven, where neither moth nor rust destroys and where thieves do not break in and steal." Unfortunately, the Securities and Exchange Commission decided that was not a sound investment strategy. I had to shut down.

Eventually, I pursued a political career. I served on the City Council in New Orleans, as mayor of Bayonne, New Jersey, and as a member of the congressional delegation from West, by God, Virginia. I became quite handy at introducing "strike-all" bills, at coming up with earmarks to fund pet projects, at hashing out new laws in smoke-filled rooms.

However, my time in office was always short-lived because of scandal. Being a Near Death Cat was attractive to the opposite sex, and there was always some kitty cat ready to lure me into a tryst or compromise my integrity.

Also, I developed political enemies, some of whom were connected to the Mob. Strange, final things began to happen to me.

I was pushed from the top of a skyscraper (or what passed for a skyscraper) in Bayonne, New Jersey, and wasn't able to right myself in the air after plunging for 20 floors. There's a saying: "It's not the fall that kills you, it's the sudden stop." As it turns out, that's correct.

Death didn't take a vacation after that. I kept going under for the count.

A 500-pound safe fell on me from a third-floor window in the Georgetown area of Washington, D.C. The funny thing was, the area was zoned for residential and low-end retail—you know, boutique shops, faux-Irish bars, restaurants where there's not much food on your plate and you can't identify it but the restaurant critics say it's good. In that kind of neighborhood, there really was no reason for someone to have a 500-pound safe in an efficiency apartment on the third floor. But, whatever. The point is the safe DID fall on me while I was trying to enjoy an espresso. By the time the waiter brought me my bill, I had been turned into flatbread with a topping of tomato sauce and arugula.

The fatalities continued. In West, by God, Virginia, I was driving a pickup truck across a crick, through a draw and on my way to a holler when the truck went up like Vesuvius. It turned out someone had planted a whole mess of dynamite under that stretch of the road and triggered it by remote control just as I passed over. Ka-pow! Blooey! Bad stuff! They found pieces of me in East, by God, Virginia. Needless to say, I didn't survive.

It was right about this time that I began to worry a little bit about my mortality. I had been using up lives like facial tissues, and I was working on No. 9. Nine! Whoo-eee. Things were getting tight.

It was time to go home, I believed, if I still had a home to go to. I hadn't communicated with either Jed or Hogarth while I had been on the road. What would they think of me? Probably from time to time, they had worried—like most friends will do—that since they hadn't heard from me I might be dead or lying in a ditch somewhere. Actually, in my case, they would have known this was an absolute certainty. *They* would have wondered whether I had been able to get up out of the ditch and carry on.

As I considered my options, I had a feeling of shame. I had been off on my own, doing whatever I wanted, living it up (and dying it down), without any regard for my friends back home. I could frame all this as a personal and spiritual quest, of course, and I intended to do exactly that if I appeared on national television. But I knew the truth. I had just been indulging myself. I had given myself over to worldly excess simply for the enjoyment of it and to build myself up in my own eyes. I had been a bad cat.

For a while, I considered giving Jed a call. Then I considered, instead, telephoning Hogarth, knowing he was less emotional and would be less likely to start blubbering with relief when he heard my voice. But then I thought, why? Wouldn't it be better just to show up and allow them to fall all over me with hugs and kisses and welcome me, now that they knew, for sure, that I was safe? Surely that would be the most emotionally satisfying course. After the bomb explosion, I pulled myself together (believe me, that was necessary), and went looking for a fast freight.

Cat and Catastrophe

I don't even remember now where I caught the first train. Wheeling, West Virginia? That would have been appropriate. In any case, I was soon motating across the great mountains and valleys of that part of the country, sharing a boxcar with some seedy types who had the same idea that I did. Get to the West at any cost.

Strangely, my on-the-bum companions weren't human. There was a lemur who had escaped from a zoo, a roof rat, a small orangutan and a colony of mice. The orangutan had been the companion of an eccentric English butler who immigrated to America with the beast disguised as his wife—fooling not only customs officers but the wife's cousins.

Our boxcar wasn't empty, but it wasn't full, either. It was stacked with cases of tomato juice, ketchup, Merlot, pickled beef hearts and beet purée, all bottled nicely for delivery to someone who intended to feed his customers with comestibles in shades of scarlet and purple. Maybe this would be dinner with a Christmas theme. How was I supposed to know?

The mice kept to themselves, and the orangutan was also standoffish once he had told his story. But the lemur and the roof rat and I got together for a real heart-to-heart as the boxcar rattled and rolled through the darkness. The lemur, unfortunately, was not very smart (his brain-to-body size ratio was smaller than that of an anthropoid primate), but he was good-hearted. The roof rat was sly, but his street smarts made up for his shiftiness. Of course, the conversation soon worked its way around to my peculiar condition.

LEMUR: So, I don't get it. How can you die and not die? Got to be one or the other. Cold or warm. Beef or bacon. Draggin' and saggin' or hoppin' and boppin'. I remember one time when I was swinging from tree to tree in Madagascar...

ROOF RAT: Don't listen to him, pal. I get the picture. You tell all these marks you've been dead, right? They want to know what it's like to be dead, right? You soak them and move on. Then you wind up dead again, and who's the wiser? No point in putting out an all-points bulletin on a dead cat, is there? Nice.

ME: Neither of you have any idea what I've been through. I've been on a spiritual quest.

LEMUR: You mean like ghosts? Crap. Are you like a ghost? Here, let me sniff your crotchal area. I have a highly developed sense of smell. Whew! No, you are real, all right.

ME: Of course I'm real, you moron. Think of me as a traveler to a distant land, which lies beyond the realm of life as we know it on earth.

ROOF RAT: Right. The old swami game. I've pulled that. You need to get yourself a turban, though. A cat turban. I used a roof rat turban. Strange look, but it worked.

ME: All right, all right. This is not a con, I told you. Why is it so hard for lower species to fathom such things?

ROOF RAT: Hey, you're lower, too, you know. Damn cats, they always think they're superior.

LEMUR: Yeah, tell him, Joey.

ROOF RAT: You are riding the rails same as us. Some bad crap happened to you. Don't tell us you are such hot feces. We know.

ME: Now, now. Of course my experiences have been humbling. I've been put to the test, again and again. That's part of my mission, I realize now. At first, I thought I had been chosen simply to survive the mystery of death so that I could infuse other beings with the knowledge of the afterlife. But as time has gone on, I've realized that I needed seasoning, that Those Above don't simply hand you wisdom, they make you earn it.

LEMUR: You mean with the cat turban. Yeah, you can probably score some bucks with that.

ME: No, no! You don't understand at all!

ROOF RAT: Oh, we understand. Do we understand! Everything that happens to you is special, because you're so great. Even ordinary whacks on the noggin are extraordinary for you, because it's part of some Big Plan. We eat thrown-away produce to survive, and you eat it to train you for the Next Big Step. You make me sick!

ME: I just don't understand how a cat with such good intentions can be taken so wrong. I really don't. I am very hurt.

ROOF RAT: Go sleep on that busted ketchup carton in the corner. Me and the lemur will sleep over here. We don't want to get smeared with your glory. You better wise up, pal.

After that, there was no more to say. I did seek out the carton, and settled down as best I could. Despite the maliciousness of the roof rat's tone, I wondered if there wasn't something in what he said. I was still wondering at 2:18 in the morning, when the freight train hit a stalled car out in the middle of Kansas and the train cars piled up like a careless child's collection of Legos.

There From Here

The first responders' voices were wild in the darkness smelling of smoke, fear-farts and the contents of busted bottles. "It's the Near Death Cat!" they cried. "It's the Near Death Cat!" Oh, no. My fame, or notoriety, had reached Minnehaha, Kansas, so much so that volunteer firemen with Budweisers on their breath could recognize me in a flashlight beam.

Even in that moment, with all the hellacious confusion, I realized I owed my butt to celebrity. No-one was trying to save the lemur, the orangutan, or the roof rat, let alone the mice. They were off somewhere in the darkness, I assumed, trying to get their battered bodies into good enough shape to struggle down to the rail bed and gasp themselves back to sentience, if they were still alive. Who knew? To my yokel rescuers, I was the only one who mattered. It was all cat, all the time. Save the tiger.

Minutes before, I had awakened to a sound like an army of Cossacks crunching a thousand beer cans. Things were sliding and crashing; I was tumbling, colliding with hard surfaces and bodies. My first thought was not, "Train wreck!" It was, "This kitty cat needs to get out from under!"

Then…nothing. My mind had slipped beneath a velvet wave of unconsciousness and I knew no more. Suddenly I came up again, with rescuers scrambling about me like crazed chinchillas.

"He's bleeding out!" one cried. "There's enough blood under my shoes to float a Cadillac!"

"Get a tourniquet around his neck!" another shouted.

Beautiful. As the blood flowed, some guy who had gotten an F in Red Cross figured the best remedy was to strangle me with an Ace bandage. I struggled weakly. I had to show them it wasn't absolutely necessary to choke me to death. The scene was grim. Blood, blood everywhere! It slopped down my chest, inundated my paws, lapped against my legs. This was it. They were right. Nine lives…and counting.

I waited for the release, the airy trip through Crystal Paradise, the canned wisdom of some flowing, vague guru. Never had the sun-baked yard back home seemed so dear, the sound of cicadas in the twilight, the taste of Long Island Iced Tea…wait, no, that was a different memory. "Fire!" someone shouted, and I caught the full contents of a fire extinguisher right in the puss. I choked and faded to black. Floating, floating, floating.

Death took a different form this time. Now there was a supreme tranquility to everything. I saw my life as it might have been. Scenes of my alternative-reality kittenhood returned. I was rolling a ball of yarn across a threadbare carpet, sucking up the contents of a split-open carton of Half-n-Half, trying to fit my tiny paw into the undulating nostril of an old geezer taking a nap. It was all so innocent. I felt as if the world were huge, and me just a micro-ball of fur with the life force inside, ready to go forth and negotiate peacefully with mice everywhere, to chase beams of sunlight, to cough up delightfully complex hair balls. Everything seemed possible.

Then I was a young cat, sharpening my claws with a premium-grade fingernail file, leaping on counters, palpating the frizzy covers of discount sofas, hearing my voice change from the soprano of adolescence to the deep rumble of early adulthood. Staying out all night in pleasantly dark alleys, knocking over garbage cans, the curses of neighbors wafting gently after me as I scampered away. Youth was wonderful. I gave voice to yowls that, to me, had the elegance of operatic arias, rising and falling through the full range of melody, even more enjoyable as my voice meshed with the smooth accompaniment of the guy down the alley shouting, "That damn cat!"

Adulthood. Marriage. A cat tuxedo. My first job, working security down at the extrusion plant. One night I found a rat trying to make off with a slice of Camembert that one of the workers had used to enhance his sardine sandwich. What a struggle. We rolled around on the ground, leaving us both huffing and puffing. He limped away, and I let him. I was so wasted that, in order to recover, I had to snatch the sandwich and eat the sardine. I saved the Camembert, though. Yes, I saved the Camembert.

Oh, if my life had only, in fact, played out like that. If only I had been a responsible cat, affectionate, a hero. Perhaps that had really been the way it was, and my memories of being a junkyard cat were incorrect. Oh, yes. That sounded good. I luxuriated in misapprehension, soothed by the balm of delusion.

My physical state mirrored that of my mind. The rhythms of the underworld were relaxing. I drifted as if I were bumping along in a warm tide, being carried toward my ultimate

destination. My ultimate destination. Who-ah. Was that going to be Cat Heaven, or Cat Hell?

Cat Heaven, if my most recent memories were on target; Cat Hell if they weren't. I knew the truth. Suddenly, a surge of anxiety tightened my throat, and I struggled to stabilize and control. I windmilled my front paws and arched my neck, but I was being pulled down, down, down…

Then, suddenly, I popped to the surface, with harsh voices rapping my eardrums. "Christ, what is this mess?"

"What do you mean? It's his blood! He's exsanguinating!"

"No, he's not. This is not his blood. It's a combination of tomato juice, ketchup, and Merlot. Not to mention beet purée. Ugh. No wonder my wife never serves beet purée."

"But look. Here's his heart! It's half-way out of his chest!"

"That's a beef heart, you fool, and it's ALL the way out of his chest. Didn't you think it was strange that his heart was bigger than his head?"

"Well, I just thought he was compassionate!"

And so it went. In the end, they cleaned my fur, patched up a few cuts, salved some contusions, put me in the hospital on a warm milk drip, and let me rest for a while. I could hear the reporters clamoring in the hallway, and the photographers practice-clicking their cameras. The prospect of facing the press filled me with dread. I realized I was no longer a prophet with a need to spread my vision. As night fell, I disconnected my IV, slipped out of bed, and escaped through the window.

The Big One

It was two weeks later. We all had assembled on Jed's porch in El Macho, and were enjoying lemonade. By "all," I mean me, Jed, Hogarth, the lemur, the roof rat and the orangutan. Yes, my train companions had survived, just as I had. After I slipped out of the hospital and vowed to continue my trip back home, I had come across them in a diner just outside Minnehaha. They were banged up, but ebullient. Surviving a tragedy creates a bond, and we were soon close.

Because of my unwanted fame, I didn't want to take regular transportation. I called Jed, and he and Hogarth showed up in the minivan two days later. We all piled in, and headed off to the land of cactuses, palm trees, and extra salsa. You would have thought that a minivan finger-painted with astrological symbols and filled with various species of animals and humans would have drawn unwanted attention, but somehow we fit right in. That's America.

The commotion had died down by the time we reached El Macho. Jed and Hogarth had prepared a place for all of us to sleep. The roof rat, of course, was most comfortable on the roof. The lemur liked to sleep hanging from the rafters. The orangutan bedded down on a broad branch near the top of the cottonwood tree in the yard. As for myself, I curled up in my old cat box. It was good to be home.

I stayed inside for the first few days while the orangutan patrolled. There was grave reason for concern that reporters, and perhaps even police investigators, would show up. All the fireworks I'd caused in El Macho before my departure would have given them reason to make a big deal out of my return. And, in a sense, I was a walking criminal case. I'd died eight times, sometimes under suspicious circumstances, so I was a strolling octuple homicide. A budding sleuth could have gotten a lifetime of experience just by sharing a saucer of milk with me.

Fame is fickle, however. After a while, it was obvious that my day in the sun was over. No media attention materialized. And that was just the way I wanted it. My career had been spectacular, no question, but it was behind me. I had come to that decision on my own and hadn't discussed it with Jed or Hogarth. But there came an afternoon, as I said, when all my friends were gathered around me on the porch, and I realized they were owed the truth.

The lemur broached the subject in his half-bright way. "So," he said, "I've been waiting for you to die again. That would be fun. Fireworks. Wailin' and weepin' and risin' from the dead. That going to happen any time soon?"

And the roof rat chimed in, in his cynical way. "Yeah, yeah. You probably need to run that con again. You know, get your personality back out on display, and garner some gelt."

The orangutan, who always showed a remarkable amount of restraint, given that he was not only one of the most intelligent primates, but one capable of showing contempt by "blowing the raspberry," remained silent.

I sipped at my lemonade. "No, my companions," I said, "that great adventure has come to an end."

Hogarth looked at me cannily. "Have you been considerin' the nature of the cosmos, based on your Near Death Experiences? And, in light of that, have you decided to devote the rest of your days to quiet study and reflection on the immensity of reality?"

Jed nodded, as if he had been thinking along similar lines.

"Not exactly," I said, quaffing lemonade and then carefully putting my glass down. "My main consideration in these last few days has been that I'm burning daylight on the last life I've got left. I know that when my next death comes, it will be The Big One." I drew in a long breath. "While that may seem a pedestrian consideration, believe me, it is not. Of course, the great cosmos does lie out there, somewhere beyond the heavens. It is equipped with some of the finest examples of crystal a cat would ever want to see. For bright tunnels, it can't be beat. Furthermore, it makes a stunning fashion statement, presenting shower curtains as a stylish mode of dress."

I took more lemonade, warming to my subject. "Frankly, though, I wish to live out my ninth life not worrying about the nature of existence on the Other Side, but focusing on the nature of existence here. I wish to spend time with my friends; I wish to play with my cat toys; I wish to have my fur soothed by my master's hand, to enjoy the smell of fresh kitty litter, to curl up at night confident that the next day will bring more of the same."

Out of the corner of my eye, I noticed Hogarth slipping into the casita. I paused for a moment or two until he re-emerged, bearing paper plates and a hot pumpkin pie. I felt fulfilled. I looked forward to what would follow: companionship, jollity, a copious amount of whipped cream.

I spread my paws, embracing all my friends with my gesture.

"This is what experience has taught me," I said. "You have to live out your life and enjoy it. You have to focus on now, and let whatever happens happen. The Other Side will present itself in good time. Now there is This Side, and it is just fine. Be of good cheer, and keep cheering every day."

I paused, angling my paw for a large chunk of pumpkin pie. "If you do that," I said, "The Big One will be nothing more than a speed bump."

THE END

How this book came to be

By Charles Kelly

Many years ago, I was considering sending a humorous cat character off to explore the Great Unknown. I had some background in this area. As a (sometimes) humorous columnist for *The Arizona Republic*, I had toyed with the creation of various personae, some of them human, some of them animal. It came to me that I might place a creature with feline complexities in the context of one of the most profound experiences in the human journey: the near-death experience.

This was not a random choice. My friend Paul Perry had written a number of books, several of them *New York Times* bestsellers, about NDEs. He had even spoken to me on occasion about the ways pets reportedly had a place in the afterlife. Many people see pets during their own near-death experiences, many more recognize their pets as friendly "ghosts" after they die, and pets often seem to be aware of extra-normal things.

What might a cat, say a fractious feline such as Dundee Blinky, experience in bridging the gap between this life and the afterlife?

I immediately set to work and tapped out a few chapters dramatizing the beginning of Dundee's adventure. Then, lazy fellow that I am, I tossed the pages on a shelf and left them there for many years.

The idea resurfaced only when I engaged my talented artist friend Kee Rash to design the cover and inside of a book called *Finnegan's Way: The Secret Power of Doing Things Badly*.

I knew that Kee was a great cat lover, and fine judge of cat character, having cared for a significant number and variety of cats. What I did not know was that he had an artistic interest in the subject. Spontaneously, as he sipped his latte, Kee said, "You know, I've always wanted to illustrate a cat book."

"Well," I rejoined, "as it happens I have half a cat book that, extended, would just serve your purpose."

Whereupon I ventured back to my writing desk, and Kee to his drawing table, and the adventures of Dundee Blinky at last came full circle, in words and pictures.

In the end, Dundee emerged as a striking character, unworthy in many ways, but also sympathetic. Kee and I found him a fine companion with which to venture into The World Beyond the World. We hope you have found him the same.

CREDITS

Photos, Dave Cruz

Charles Kelly is a former reporter for *The Arizona Republic*. During his career, he investigated the 1976 contract murder of *Republic* reporter Don Bolles, located several missing heirs, and helped a wrongly convicted American tugboat captain get out of a Mexican prison. He is the author of the novel *Pay Here*, issued by Point Blank Press, the story "The Eighth Deadly Sin," published in the collection *Phoenix Noir* issued by Akashic Books, and the self-help book *Finnegan's Way: The Secret Power of Doing Things Badly*. His biography of an amnesiac hard-boiled novelist, *Gunshots in Another Room: The Forgotten Life of Dan J. Marlowe*, has been called a "masterpiece" by Ed Gorman, the legendary mystery author and editor. Kelly lives in Scottsdale, Arizona.

The illustrations for this book were created by Kee Rash, graphic designer and artist who, in addition to drawing cats, likes baseball, coffee, and any kind of good music. A native of Arizona, he and his wife, Melanie, live in Phoenix, where they care for a colony of around 10 cats. "The cats showed up at our house and decided we were okay to live with," Kee explained. "They provide great company and all have different personalities. However, I have yet to meet a cat that talks like Dundee."

www.ingramcontent.com/pod-product-compliance
Lightning Source LLC
Chambersburg PA
CBHW051659040426
42446CB00009B/1207